This book belongs to:

_ _ _ _ _ _ _ _ _ _ _

This print run of Arlo's Adventures There and Back
has been funded by Great Western Railway - www.gwr.com

GWR | Great
Western
Railway

For Madison

ISBN 978-1-3999-2652-2

Copyright ©
Bessie Matthews, 2022 all images and text
All rights reserved
Published by Community Rail Education Network

Without limiting the rights under copyright reserved above,
no part of this publication may be reproduced without the prior written permission of the copyright owner.

Arlo is leaving to visit his friends, Duskie and Moss.
They live in the town where Arlo used to live, just two stops away on the train.

Today is the first time he will be travelling all by himself, there and back.

Can you help Arlo and his friends make safe choices around the railway?

1

Arlo finds himself at a level crossing.
He notices an amber light appear on the Wig-Wag signal.
This means the barriers are about to come down because there
is a train coming!

What should Arlo do?

2

Arlo is a really fast runner! Should he run across to the other side before the barriers come down?

Turn to Page 4.

Should Arlo wait for the barriers to come down and the train to pass? It will only take a couple of minutes.

Turn to Page 5.

3

"If I run across," Arlo thinks to himself, "I could get seriously hurt - or worse!"

Running through an active level crossing is very dangerous.

Remember: Trains can come from both directions. You should always wait for the lights to stop flashing and the barriers to raise before crossing

4

Have a look at the next page to see the best way to keep safe at a level crossing.

"I can wave to all the people on the train while I wait!"

Well done! Keeping a good distance from the barriers while the trains pass is the best way to stay safe around the railway.

Arlo has arrived at the railway station.
There is a big yellow line painted on the floor near the edge of
the platform. The train is about to arrive and there are other
people waiting too.

What should Arlo do?

Should Arlo stand in front of the yellow line so he can get on the train first?

Turn to Page 8.

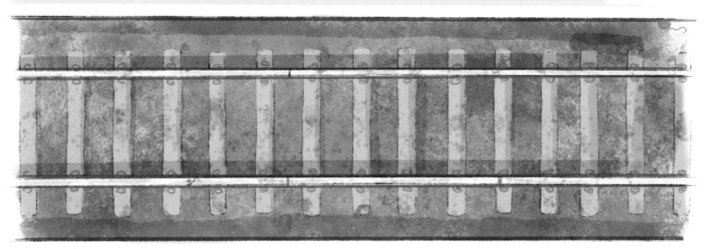

Should Arlo stand behind the yellow line and away from the edge?

Turn to Page 9.

"If I stand in front of the yellow line," Arlo thinks to himself, "I could get seriously hurt - or worse!"

Standing too close to the platform edge is very dangerous.

Trains can travel really fast through stations, up to 125mph - that's quicker than a cheetah!
This speed can create strong winds that might push or pull you.

8

Have a look at the next page to see the best way to keep safe on a station platform.

"I can see the driver and they can see me!"

Well done! Standing behind the yellow line and away from the platform edge is the best way to stay safe around the railway.

It's kind to allow other passengers to get off the train before you get on.

Arlo is on board the train!
He loves to look out of the window during train journeys.
There is an empty seat by a window, but the longest windows
are on the doors.

What should Arlo do?

Should Arlo stand up against
the doors to look out of the
long window?

Turn to Page 12.

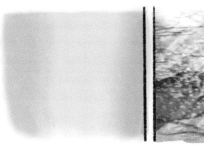

Should Arlo find a seat?
There's one with a view!

Turn to Page 13.

"If I fall over," Arlo thinks to himself, "I could get hurt – or hurt others!"

Standing without holding a handrail can be very dangerous.

Trains can stop suddenly. If you're not holding on or sitting sensibly, you could fall or bump in to other passengers.

Have a look at the next page to see the best way to keep safe on the train.

"I can eat a snack while looking out of the window!"

Well done! Staying seated or holding on to handrails is the best way to stay safe while on a moving train.

It's kind to keep away from the doors to let other passengers get on or off the train safely.

Arlo has arrived safely at the station where his friends are waiting for him.

"Hello Duskie! Hello Moss!"

"Hi Arlo," smiles Duskie. "I've brought my new football."

What should Arlo do?

"Shall we cross the tracks?" asks Moss. "It's the quickest way."

Turn to Page 16.

Should Arlo and his friends use the footbridge to get to the other side of the station?

Turn to Page 17.

"If we jump down on to the tracks," Arlo says. "We could get seriously hurt - or worse!"

Running across the tracks is very dangerous.
There could be an electric Conductor Rail that powers trains with up to 750 volts of electricity - that's enough to light up a street!
If you touch this live rail, you would get a big electric shock and terrible burns.

16

Have a look at the next page to see the best way to keep safe when changing platforms.

"We can see the whole station from up here!"

Well done! Using footbridges, underpasses or foot crossings is the best way to stay safe around the railway.

Arlo and his friends spend hours playing lots of different games in the park. Their favourite game is football.
Duskie has a very strong kick and accidentally kicks the ball over the fence! It lands on the train tracks.

What should Arlo do?

Should Arlo get ready to catch the ball when Duskie throws it over the fence?

Turn to Page 20.

Should Arlo and his friends tell railway staff at the station about their ball?

Turn to Page 21.

19

"If you go to get the ball," Arlo tells Duskie, "You could get seriously hurt - or worse!"

Going on or near the railway line is very dangerous.
Some trains are quieter than you think, all trains are slow to stop.
Trains can come from either direction at any time, during day or night.

Have a look at the next page to see the best way to keep safe if there's something on or near the tracks.

"Excuse me, our ball has fallen on the railway line."

Well done! Telling railway staff about items dropped on the train tracks is the best way to stay safe around the railway.

After a great day, it's time for Arlo to go home.
Duskie and Moss decide to stay with him until his train arrives.
Their legs are tired but the platform is really busy and there's nowhere to sit down.

What should Arlo do?

22

Should Arlo sit at the edge of the platform with Moss?

Turn to Page 24.

Should Arlo and his friends stand and wait away from the platform's edge?

Turn to Page 25.

"If we sit with our legs over the platform edge," Arlo tells his friends, "We could get seriously hurt - or worse!"

Sitting over the edge of the platform is very dangerous.
It's easy to lose your balance and fall on to the track.

Not all trains passing through stations are advertised on screens or over station announcements.

Have a look at the next page to see the best way to keep safe with friends on a platform.

"Goodbye, Arlo! Have a safe journey home!"

Well done! Keeping a good distance from the edge of the
platform is the best way to stay safe around the railway.

25

It's the end of another pleasant journey. Arlo is almost home. As he is leaving the station, he notices a balloon caught up in the wires that run along above the tracks.
The balloon's string is blowing over the platform.

What should Arlo do?

26

Dad would love this balloon. Should Arlo try to get the balloon down?

Turn to Page 28.

Should Arlo tell railway staff at the station? They'll know what to do.

Turn to Page 29.

"If I touch the balloon's string," Arlo thinks to himself, "I could get seriously hurt - or worse!"

Making contact with the wires above the tracks is very dangerous. The overhead line equipment powers trains with up to 25,000 volts of electricity.
If you touch this wire, or anything on it, you would get a big electric shock and terrible burns.
Have a look at the next page to see the best way to keep safe if you notice something on the overhead lines.

"Thank you for telling us! We will work on getting the balloon down safely."

Well done! Telling railway staff about anything stuck in the Overhead Line Equipment is the best way to stay safe around the railway.

It's always safer to ask for help.
Railway staff have special tools for almost any task!

Arlo puts his ticket in to the ticket gate at the station exit. To his surprise, it reappears as the gate opens.

"I'm going to keep this ticket forever" Arlo thinks to himself, "to remember such a great day!"

Arlo can't wait for his next adventure on the train, all by himself, there and back.

Glossary

Definitions of some of the words found in this book.

Level Crossing

Where railway crosses over road or path. There are lots of different types of crossing but they're treated all the same! When a train is coming, stand back and wait.

Wig-Wag Signal

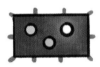

You can find these at some level crossings. They can be landscape or portrait. You might even spot them around tunnels, airfields, special bridges and even by emergency service depots like the fire station. When they flash, they mean KEEP CLEAR.

Yellow Line

An indication of where the most safe place to stand is: Behind the yellow line! Some yellow lines are bumpy so that people who may not be able to see can feel where they need to be to stay safe.

Ticket and Ticket Gate

Tickets can be card-like, the same as Arlo's, or they can be in the form of a long roll of paper, a print out from a computer or even on a mobile phone! Every ticket is unique and it's important to look after yours, whatever type that may be, while you're travelling. All tickets are used to open the ticket gates, or barriers, at stations.

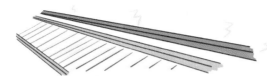

Conductor Rail

Also known as Third Rail, Live Rail, Electric Rail and sometimes The Juice Rail.
This special rail supplies electricity to most trains in many areas around the UK via a
train 'shoe'. It looks just like any other rail but it's not to be treated the same.
Always treat the tracks as electrified!

  ## 750 volts

A volt is a measurement of electricity and there can be up to 750 volts DC in a conductor rail.
DC stands for Direct Current, ,which means the electricity is flowing in one direction.
It's a sticky type of electric, meaning if you were to touch the Conductor Rail, you would
stick to it.

Overhead Wires

Another method of powering electric trains. They can be called Overhead Wires, Overhead Line
Equipment (OLE/OHLE) or perhaps even The Knitting Above. Electric trains draw power
through their pantograph, which is the stick you might see on the roof!

 ## 25,000 volts

Sometimes shortened to 25kV, is how many volts run through the OHLE. Unlike the
conductor rail, the electricity in these wires sometimes change direction. This is called
Alternating Current, or AC. You won't find sticky electricity here. If you were to come
in to contact with the wires above train tracks, it would blast you far away with a big
BANG!

You can read more about Arlo and his daily life online:

@ArloAdventures

About Bessie

Arlo's best friend is Bessie, and she comes up with ideas for all his adventures. She lives in Hampshire with her partner, her pack of dogs and any other animal that chooses to live with her. When she's not watching films, cuddling puppies or staying safe with Arlo, she's driving trains around the UK's second biggest container terminal.

Both Bess and Arlo love the railway and want to make sure everyone knows how to stay safe.

-Mike Roberts, Railway Chaplain and friend.

FINDING A FUTURE FOR VULNERABLE CHILDREN

The story in this book demonstrates that railway systems are places of adventure and experiences – and play a huge part in all of our lives whether we live near them, travel on them or work within them. It is vital that together we make sure they remain safe places for all that pass through them and we hope the readers of this book will help us do that by supporting the work of Railway Children.

RAILWAY CHILDREN IS AN INTERNATIONAL CHARITY THAT HAS CHANGED THE LIVES OF MORE THAN 325,000 CHILDREN OVER THE LAST 25 YEARS.

The charity fights for children around the world that have no one else to protect and care for them. Children who are forced to survive on the streets and around the railways in India, Africa and here in the UK where they often put themselves in danger using public transport to run away from home.

In the UK, Railway Children has a unique partnership with British Transport Police and takes referrals from them of young people they find at risk on the network.

Officers identify around 10,000 such children every year and by working closely with the police and train companies, the charity is able to offer support to some of the most hard to reach and vulnerable children in the UK.

Often these children are using the rail system as they are desperate to escape difficult homes or sometimes they are on their way to meet strangers who are planning to take advantage of them. Many are simply falling through the cracks in the system and some are suffering through bullying, loneliness and poor mental health.

Wherever the charity finds these children, and whatever they are facing, they use the same approach to make sure they are safe from harm – always trying to reach them as soon as possible and make sure they are safe. Then they work with the child, their family, their school or even their entire community to make sure they do not end up in danger again. They help each individual reach their full potential, thrive in a safe environment and carve out a future worth looking forward to.

WITH YOUR HELP RAILWAY CHILDREN CAN CONTINUE TO KEEP THESE YOUNG PEOPLE SAFE FOR MANY YEARS TO COME.

PLEASE GIVE WHATEVER YOU CAN. THANK YOU.

TO DONATE OR
FIND OUT MORE:

RAILWAY
children
Fighting for street children

With massive thanks to Karen Bennett.

Without you, none of this would have
been possible.